# FINE IRISH CROCHET LACE

## Cartier-Bresson

DOVER PUBLICATIONS, INC.
New York

*Bibliographical Note*

*Fine Irish Crochet Lace*, first published by Dover Publications, Inc., in 1994, is a republication of *How to Make Baby Irish Crochet Lace (2nd Album): A Practical Method with 53 Illustrations*, originally published by Cartier-Bresson, Paris, n.d. One page of advertising has been omitted. A new Publisher's Note has been written for this edition.

*Library of Congress Cataloging-in-Publication Data*

Guipure d'Irlande Fine. English.
    Fine Irish crochet lace / Cartier-Bresson.
        p.    cm.
    Originally published: How to make baby Irish crochet lace. 2nd album. Paris, France : Printed by Cartier-Bresson, [193-?]. (Collection C.B.).
    ISBN 0-486-27874-3 (pbk.)
    1. Irish crochet lace.   2. Lace and lace making—Patterns.   I. Cartier-Bresson (Firm)   II. Title.
TT805.I74G85    1994
746.2'2—dc20                                                                93-42335
                                                                                CIP

Manufactured in the United States of America
Dover Publications, Inc., 31 East 2nd Street, Mineola, N.Y. 11501

# Publisher's Note

Irish crochet was developed in the mid-nineteenth century as a less expensive imitation of Venetian needlepoint lace. It soon became prized in its own right, and a great many books and magazines offering patterns for Irish crochet appeared. The work featured in this book, originally published around the turn of the century by a manufacturer of threads for crochet, is particularly dainty and delicate. The original title of the book was *How to Make Baby Irish Crochet Lace*, a reference to the fineness of the work rather than to its end use.

In Irish crochet, separate motifs are made, then joined with an openwork background to form a variety of articles. Several of these articles are illustrated in the book. Instructions are also given for a number of edgings which are just as useful today as they were at the turn of the century.

Two to three different sizes of thread are required for the patterns—a fine thread for the motifs, a slightly thicker thread used as a "foundation cord" or padding and, for some designs, an even finer thread for the background.

Extremely fine thread—No. 160 in some cases—was originally called for in the patterns. Not surprisingly, the specific threads called for are no longer being made, and the range of thread sizes available is much more limited now than it was when the book was originally published. D.M.C., one of the largest thread manufacturers, makes cotton crochet threads in sizes up to No. 100, with No. 70 being the finest thread commonly found in stores. Some distributors specializing in lacemaking supplies stock cotton threads as fine as No. 180 and linen threads as fine as No. 140, but these threads are still difficult to locate. In addition, many modern crocheters find such fine threads difficult to work. The tendency today, therefore, is to use thicker threads for the work, for example No. 5 pearl cotton for the foundation, No. 30 cotton for the motifs and No. 70 for the background. Before beginning a project, it is a good idea to make a small sample with the thread and hook that you plan to use. If your stitches are loose and untidy, use a smaller hook. If they appear crowded, use a larger hook. Keep making samples until you get the look you want.

The instructions are reproduced here exactly as originally printed, and are likely to appear somewhat strange to modern eyes. The terminology is British, and not the same as that used in the United States today. Generally, the names of the stitches have all shifted by one—what is referred to as a double crochet in the book is known to American crocheters as a single crochet, the book's treble crochet is our double crochet and so on. A chart listing the modern American equivalents to the older British terms is given at the end of this Note.

In addition, the instructions will appear very abbreviated to today's crocheters. When this book was published, it was taken for granted that the reader already knew the basic stitches of the work, so the instructions were much less specific than instructions today. If you have difficulty understanding a pattern, study the photograph carefully—the stitches show up clearly in most of them. This book is the second volume on Irish crochet published by Cartier-Bresson. Two of the articles shown, the "Baby Irish Lace" on page 18 and the "Sprig with three Points" on page 58, refer to fillings and/or picot edgings explained in the first volume. Since these articles are particularly attractive, we decided to include them even though we do not have access to the first volume. By studying the photographs carefully, you should be able to substitute one of the fillings and edgings described in this volume.

MARY CAROLYN WALDREP
*Needlework Editor*
*Dover Publications, Inc.*

## Stitch Conversion Chart

| BRITISH NAME | CURRENT AMERICAN NAME |
| --- | --- |
| chain | chain |
| double stitch | single crochet |
| treble | half double crochet |
| double treble | double crochet |
| tight stitch | slip stitch |
| slip stitch | slip stitch |
| miss | skip |

# Baby Irish Crochet Lace

This volume continues our 1st Album *How to make Irish Crochet Lace* in which the directions for the different stitches of this lace have been given.

Baby Irish Crochet Lace is worked as the other but it is finer. Finer thread is used and round the sprigs which are smaller, rows of stitches with picots are usually worked instead of the filling.

Baby Irish Lace has always been very much in vogue for trimming babies and children's garments and also lingerie. It is also very effective for trimming blouses and can be mixed with other kinds of lace or with embroidery.

## Materials required for the Making of Baby Irish Lace

**Crochet Needle.** — Irish Crochet Lace is worked with the same steel crochet needle which is used for ordinary lace.

**Thread.** — A special cotton is used, *the Fil d'Irlande Brillanté C·B, à la Croix* (Art. 220), on reels of 25 grammes. This thread can be had in sizes n$^{os}$ 30 (the coarsest), 40, 50, 60, 70, 80, 90, 100, 120, 140, 160, 180, 200 (the finest). The sizes most usually employed for Baby Irish Lace are 100, 120, 140, 160.

**Foundation Cord.** — The foundation cord is a coarser cotton or cord than the working thread and is used as a padding for certains sprigs. The cotton used for this cord is the *Cordonnet 6 fils C·B, à la Croix* (Art. 20), balls of 25 or 10 grammes. The size of cotton used as a cord for Baby Irish Lace is usually n° 5.

### OBSERVATION

In order to make the directions clearer the springs shown in the illustrations have been worked with coarse cotton (n° 60). But the sizes of the thread and cotton required for working each of these sprigs in their ordinary size is given with every design.

The fine laces are given in the size they are to be made and the n° of the thread which has been used for working them is indicated.

### ABBREVIATIONS

The following abbreviations are used in this album:

| | | | |
|---|---|---|---|
| Chain-stitch . . . . . | ch. | Double treble. . . . . | d. tr. |
| Double stitch. . . . . | d. st. | Picot. . . . . . . . . | p. |
| Treble. . . . . . . . . | tr. | Turn. . . . . . . . . . | t. |
| Alternately. . . . . . . . . | | alt. | |

# PICOTS

## Picot n° 1

FIG. N° 1

On a chain or on the lace, work:

*1st row.* — 1 tr. — 2 ch. — 1 tr. into the 3rd nearest st.

*2nd row.* — * 3 d. st. into each hole — after the 3rd group of 3 st. t. — 4 ch. — 1 tr. into the 3rd nearest st. — 4 ch. — 1 d. st. into the 3rd st. — T. — Into the first half of the loop — 5 d. st. — 1 p. of 4 ch. — 2 d. st. Into the 2nd half of the loop — 2 d. st. — 1 p. — 5 d. st.

Repeat always from *.

## Picot n° 2

FIG. N° 2

On a chain or on the lace, work:

*1st row.* — 1 tr. — 3 ch. — 1 tr. into the 4th nearest st.

*2nd row.* — * 5 d. st. on the 4 ch. — T. — 4 ch. — 2 tr. separated by 4 ch. on the 5th nearest st. — 4 ch. — 1 d. st. into the 5th nearest st. — T. — On each loop — 3 d. st. — 1 p. of 4 ch. — 3 d. st. — 1 d. st. on the lower chain.

Into the next row of open spaces which forms the edge — 3 d. st. — 1 p. — 3 d. st.

Repeat from *.

On a chain or on the edge of the lace or insertion, work:

*1*<sup></sup> *st row.* — 1 tr. — 2 ch. — 1 tr. into the 3<sup>rd</sup> nearest st.

*2*<sup></sup> *nd row.* — * 3 d. st. over one of the open spaces of the previous row — on the 2<sup>nd</sup> open space, 2 d. st. — 1 p. (5 ch. joined by 1 tight st. worked on the last d. st.) — 2 d. st. — on the 3<sup>rd</sup>

## Picot n° 3

open space 2 d. st. — 9 ch. — t. to join to the 4<sup>th</sup> nearest st. after the p. — T.

For a plain loop, work — 14 d. st. on the 9 ch.

For a loop with p., work — 4 d. st. — 1 p. made as above — 3 d. st. — 1 p. — 3 d. st. — 1 p. — 3 d. st. — 1 p. — 4 d. st. -- To finish — 1 d. st. on the lower ch.

Repeat from *.

# Picot n° 4

On a chain or on the lace, work :
*1st row.* — 1 tr. — 3 ch. — 1 tr. into the 4th nearest st.
*2nd row.* — *3 times — 4 d. st. into each ole. — T. — 5 ch. —
1 d. st. on the 4th nearest st. — T.
Into the 1st loop — 3 d. st. — 1 p. of 4 ch. — 2 d. st. — then
6 ch. (the 5 last st. joined to form 1 p.) 2 ch. — On the remaining loop — 2 d. st. — 1 p. — 3 d. st. — 1 d. st. into the hole
where the scallop was begun.
Repeat always from*

# Picot n° 5

Fig. n° 5

On a chain or on the work, crochet :
*1st row.* — 1 tr. — 3 ch. — 1 tr. into the 4th nearest st.
*2nd row.* — * 4 d. st. over each hole of the previous row —
4 times. — Then t. — 4 ch. — pass the thread 3 times over the
needle — into the 4th nearest st. begin 1 tr. keeping the last
thread on the needle — pass the thread over the needle twice
again to work into the 4th following nearest st. a 2nd tr. which
yon finish with the 1st one.
With the thread remaining on the needle, work 1 tr. above —
then 8 ch. — 1 tr. worked at the junction of the tr. already made.
— It forms a cross. — 4 ch. — 1 d. st. into the 4th nearest st. of
the edge. — T.

Into the 1st loop — 5 d. st. — 1 p. of 4 ch. -- 2 d. st. into the 2nd loop (the top one) -- 2 d. st. — 1 p. — 4 p. st. — 1 d. — 4 d. st. — 1 p. — 2 d. st. — and into the 3rd loop — 2 d. st. — 1 p. — 4 d. st. — 1 d. st. into the open space where the loops were begun.

Repeat from*.

# Irish Picot

On a chain or on the lace, work :

*1st row*. — 1 tr. — 2 ch. — 1 tr. into the 3rd nearest st.

*2nd row*. — 5 times 3 d. st. into each open space of the previous row. — T. — *6 ch. — 1 d. st. into the 4th nearest st. — Repeat twice from*. — T. — 3 d. st. — 1 p. of 4 ch. — 1 d. st. — then 6 ch. — 1 st. into the middle loop — 3 ch. — 1 tr. into the following loop. — T. —6 ch. — 1 d. st. into the loop — 3 ch. and 1 d. st. to get back to the loop already filled. — On the 2 ch. — 3 d. st. — 1 p. — 2 d. st. — On the top loop — 3 d. st. — 1 p. — 2 d. st. — 1 p. — 3 d. st. — On the tr. which forms a loop — 2 d. st. — 1 p. — 3 d. st. — On the last loop — 1 d. st. — 1 p. — 3 d. st. — 1 d. st. into the open space which has been worked into previously.

# Screen Picot

FIG. N° 7

On a chain or on the lace, work :

1st *row*. — 1 tr. — 3 ch. — 1 tr. into the 4th st.

2nd *row*. — Beginning from the left — *10 ch. joined to the 2nd nearest tr. — T. — 3 d. st. on the foundation ch. — Repeat always from*.

3rd *row*. — Beginning from the right — 13 d. st. on the 1st open space — on the following one, 5 d. st. — then 10 ch. — join to the 5th nearest st. of the 1st group — 15 d. st. on the loop — 4 d. st. on the open space.

18 ch. — Join to the 4th st. after the junction of the 1st loop — 10 d. st.

For a small loop, work : — *8 ch. — join to the 2nd nearest st., and in the small loop thus formed work : — 5 d. st. — 1 p. of 4 ch. — 4 d. st. — 1 p. — 5 d. st. — close the small loop with 1 tight st. — then 4 d. st. on the large loop. — Repeat twice from*.

There are 3 small loops on the top of the large loop — then 8 d. st. — 4 d. st. on the open space of the edge which has already been worked into.

Always repeat.

# Fan Picot

FIG. N° 8

On a row of ch. or on the lace, work :

*1st row*. — 1 tr. — 3 ch. — 1 tr. into the 3rd st.

*2nd row*. — 3 times. — 4 d. st. into each hole — 3 d. st. into the next hole. — T.

10 ch. — join by 1 d. st. to the 7th nearest st. — T. — 11 d. st. on the ch. — then 2 d. st. on the edge — 1 into the hole which has already been worked into and 1 into the next. — T.

4 ch. — 11 times — 1 tr. — 1 d. st. — join with 1 d. st. to the 4th st. of the edge. — T.

2 d. st. into each open space — and 2 st. on the edge into the hole which has already been worked into.

Always repeat this row.

*3rd row*. — On the scallops — 6 ch. — 1 d. st. into the 3rd — at the top twice into the 2nd st. — between the scallops — once on the 4th st.

# SMALL SPRIGS

Materials required
for the work :

FOUNDATION
CORD :

*Cordonnet 6 fils
à la Croix*
*C·B n° 5*

❧

THREAD :

*Fil d'Irlande
Brillante*
*C·B*
*n° 120-140*

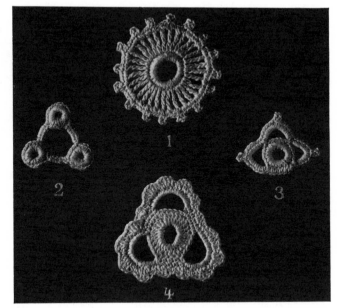

FIG. Nº 9

## Nº 1. Rosace

Join the cord into a ring and over it, work :
*1st row*. — 32 d. st. — join the last to the 1st.
*2nd row*. — 5 ch. — always 1 d. tr. — 1 ch. — there should be 32 d. tr. — the first 5 st. stand for 1 d. tr.
*3rd row*. — 2 d. st. into each open space — after each 2nd open space, work — 1 p., that is to say 4 ch. joined with 1 d. st.

## Nº 2. Triangle of small rings

Wind the cord 3 times on a very small mesh, and over it work for a small ring — 20 d. tight st. — finish off the thread.
At the end of a 2nd similar ring, work — 4 ch. which are joined to the 1st ring — cover the ch. with 5 d. st. and finish off with 1 d. st. on the ring.

For the 3rd small ring — after the 5th d. st. join with 4 ch. to the 5th free st. of the 2nd ring — cover with 5 ch. Then on the ring, 15 d. st. — join the 5th free st. of the 1st ring — cover with 5 d. st. and finish off with 1 st. on the ring.

## N° 3. Three points

Wind the cord twice round a mesh and over it, work 24 d. st. join with 1 tight st.

With the cord — 1 d. st. on the ring — over the cord alone to form a loop — 6 d. st. — 1 p. closed with 4 ch. — 6 d. st. — 1 d. st. in the 6th st. of the ring.

Repeat twice — that is to say 3 loops — then 6 d. st. on the ring which forms the edge.

## N° 4. Triangle with scallopped edge

Begin with 10 ch. joined into a ring.

*1st row.* — 3 ch. — then 20 tr. — join to the 3rd ch.

*2nd row.* — 5 d. st. — 10 ch. — miss 4 st. of the ring and repeat twice.

*3rd row.* — 5 d. st. on the 5 st. of the previous row — 18 d. st. on the 10 ch.

*4th row.* — Always 1 d. st. — 1 slip st. — 2 tr. into the same st. — 1 tr. — 1 slip st. The edge is scalloped.

# SPRIGS

Materials required
for the work :

FOUNDATION
CORD :

*Cordonnet 6 fils
à la Croix*

*C·B. n° 5*

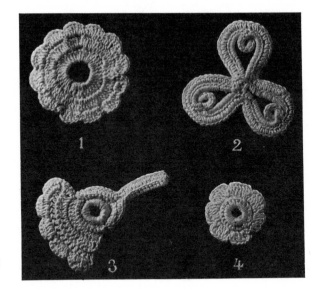

❧

THREAD :

*Fil d'Irlande
Brillanté*
*C·B n° 120-140*

## N° 1. Ring with treble stitches

On 12 ch. joined into a ring, work :

*1st row.* — 36 tr. — To stand for the 1st tr. — 3 ch. and finish off with a tight st. on the 3rd st.

*2nd row.* — 2 tr. on each tr. of the previous row — that is to say 72 tr.

*3rd row.* — 1 d. st. — 1 tr. — 1 tr. — 2 tr. — 1 tr. — 1 tr. — Always repeat and it makes 12 scallops round the ring.

## N° 2. Three Spirals

Over the cord work first :

15 d. st. — then 12 d. st. — Pass the cord when filled under to form a loop and join to the 12th st. from the needle — 15 d. st. — Join the last st. to the beginning with 1 st. across the 2.

Repeat twice.

Then always with the cord — 1 d. st. on the st. of the previous row. Take the back loop to form the rib.

# N° 3. Palm Leaf

Wind the cord twice round a small mesh and over it work :

*1st row.* — 28 d. st. formed into a ring by joining the last to the 1st T.

*2nd row.* — Without the cord — on the ring — 14 d. st. worked into the back loop. — T.

*3rd row.* — 3 ch. — 2 tr. on the nearest d. st. — then 1 tr. on each st. and 2 tr. into the st. before the last — 1 tr. on the last st. — Always work on the back loop. — T.

*4th row.* — As the previous row — increasing at the beginning and at the end. — T.

*5th row.* — Also same as the 3rd row — there should be 20 tr. — T.

*6th row.* — 1 d. st. — 3 times 2 tr. into each st. — 1 d. st. — The edge is scalloped with 5 round scallops.

Work d. st. along the side.

Round the ring on the part which has not been worked on previously, crochet — 1 row of ribbed d. st. — T. — Taking the cord again, always with ribbed d. st. reach the middle of the ring.

On the cord alone for the stem — 12 d. st. — T. — Work back on these st. and complete the round on the ring.

# N° 4. Small round sprig

Wind the cord twice round the handle of the needle and over it, work :

*1st row.* — 24 d. st. — join the last to the 1st. — Turn the work over as the wrong side of the centre ring should be the right side of the work.

*2nd row.* — 24 d. st. worked tightly without passing the thread over the needle — work into the back loop of the previous row.

*3rd row.* — *Always 1 d. st. — 1 ch. — then 2 tr. into the nearest st. — 1 tr. — 2 tr. into the same st. — 1 ch. — 1 d. st. on the following st. — Repeat 6 times from*. — That is to say 7 scallops round the ring.

# SPRIGS

FOUNDATION CORD :
*Cordonnet 6 fils à la Croix*
*C·B n° 5*

FIG. N° II

THREAD :
*Fil d'Irlande Brillanté*
*C·B n° 120-140*

## N° 1. Medallion

Wind the cord 3 times round the crochet needle, and over it work 22 tr., join and leave the cord. — Then all round 1 row of d. st.

The small centre ring is complete — finish off the thread. — Work another similar ring which you join to the 1st with d. st. and p. — 6 ch. — 1 d. st. into the 2nd st. — 1 ch. — Join with 1 d. st. to the 1st small ring.

Repeat twice joining alt. to one ring and to the other. — Then 5 ch. — 1 d. tr. after the last p. — 1 ch. — *1 d. tr. on the nearest free st. of the ring — 1 ch. — 1 tr. — On the 2nd nearest st. — twice — 1 ch. 1 tr. without any space in between. — Always tr. st. with ch. — after missing 1 st. on the ring — work 8 times tr. st. without missing any — then 1 space — 3 tr. without space — 1 space — : d. tr. separated by a ch. on the st. before and after the p. — Repeat round the 2nd ring from *.

*2nd row*. — Always 2 d. st. into each space.

*3rd row*. — Always 1 tr. separated by 2 ch. on the 2nd nearest st. — To form the ring work 3 times — 3 tr. without any space in between, inserting 1 tr. with a space. There should be 42 tr. · all round.

*4th row*. — Always 3 d. st. into each hole. — At each end only 1 p.

## N° 2. Star

On 12 d. st. joined into a ring, work :

*1st row*. — 36 tr.

*2nd row*. — 6 ch. — 1 d. st. into the 3rd nearest st. — Repeat 10 times.

*3rd row*. — 6 ch. — 1 d. st. into the loop.

*4th row*. — For a small scallop. On the ch. — 1 d. st. — 1 slip — st. — 5 tr. — 1 slip — st. — 1 d. st. — There should be 12 scallops and finish off the thread.

## N° 3. Triangle with open work edge

On 10 ch. joined into a ring, work:

*1st row*. — 27 tr.

*2nd row*. — 5 d. st. on the 5 nearest st. of the ring — 10 ch. — miss 4 st. of the ring and repeat twice.

*3rd row*. — 5 d. st. on those of the previous row — 18 tr. on the ch. — Repeat.

*4th row*. — Always — 1 tr. — 1 ch. — 1 tr. into the 2nd nearest st. To form the rounded edge omit missing 1 st. 3 times at each round.

# Baby Irish Lace

## FOR LAYETTE OR LINGERIE

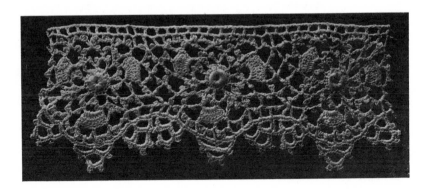

FOUNDATION CORD :
*Cordonnet 6 fils à la Croix*
*C·B n° 5*

FIG. N° 12

THREAD :
*Fil d'Irlande Brillante*
*C·B n° 120*

Over the cord which has been wound 4 times round the handle of the needle, work :

*1st row.* — 20 slip — st. — For 1 slip — st. pass the thread over the needle and take the loop and thread as usual, but draw both through at the same time.

*2nd row.* — T. — 10 times — 1 d. st. (for an arch, 6 ch. — 1 d. st. into the 2nd ch. — 6 ch. and 1 d. st. — 1 ch.) always 1 d. st. into the 2nd nearest st. of the ring.

*3rd row.* — * 1 cluster — (for a cluster, 5 ch. — 1 d. st. between the 2 p. of the nearest arch. — T. — 3 ch. — 8 tr. — T. — 1 ch. — 1 d. st. on the tr.). — Then a plain arch, that is to say : 6 ch. — 1 d. st. into the 2nd st. — 1 ch. — 1 d. st. into the arch which has already been worked into but after the p. — then 2 d. arches.
Repeat twice from *.
There should be 3 clusters with arches in between.

*4th row.* — Always d. arches — stick your needle into the beginning, the middle and the end of the cluster.

At the end of the row join with plain arches 4 arches to the 4 corresponding arches of the previous sprig and break off the thread.

*For the edge :*

Always 1 tr. — 2 ch. — 1 tr. — work 1 d. tr. at the junction of 2 sprigs.

Then 1 tr. — 2 ch. — 1 tr. taken on the ch. of the previous row.

*For the scalloped edge :*

Always 1 tr. before 1 p. — 2 ch. — 1 tr. after the same p.

You make a scalloped edge with p. by working always regularly a scallop at each point.

*Picot :*

See fig. n° 12 of the 1st album : " How to make Irish Crochet Lace ".*

*See Publisher's Note

DÉMONSTRATION

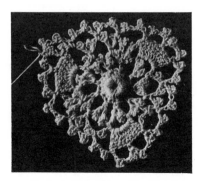

FIG. N° 13

# Lace with small Scallops

## WITHOUT PICOT

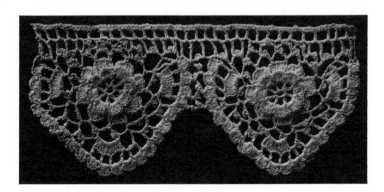

FOUNDATION
CORD :
*Cordonnet 6 fils
à la Croix*
*C·B n° 5*

THREAD :
*Fil d'Irlande
Brillanté*
*C·B n° 120*

Begin the centre of each sprig with a small rose.

For a rose with 8 leaves.

On 6 ch. joined into a ring :

*1st row.* — 5 ch. — 1 tr. — 2 ch. — repeat 6 times, to have 7 tr. — and 1 tight st. on the 3rd of the 5 ch., to form 8 tr.

*2nd row.* — 8 leaflets. — For a leaflet into each hole of the previous row — 1 d. st. — 1 slip — st. — 5 tr. — 1 slip — st. — 1 d. st.

*3rd row.* — 1 tr. worked underneath, on each tr. of the 1st row 3 ch.

*4th row.* — 8 leaflets. — For a leaflet, into each hole — 1 d. st. — 1 slip — st. — 7 tr. — 1 slip — st. — 1 d. st.

The rose is complete.

*5th row.* — 1 arch. — (6 ch. — 1 d. st. into the 2nd st. to form 1 p. — 3 ch.) 1 d. st. — Stick the needle alt. once and twice above each leaflet — there should be 12 arches.

*6th row.* — 1 arch — 1 cluster — 6 ch. — 1 d. st. into the nearest arch. — T. — 6 ch. — 1 d. st. on the previous st. —3 ch. — 11 tr. on the 6 ch. which have been worked one way and back — 1 arch. — 1 d. st. into the arch which has been previously worked into — then 2 arches — repeat — that is to say 3 clusters. — After the arch following the 3rd cluster. — T.

*7th row.* — 8 ch. — 1 tr. before the cluster and twice in succession — 1 tr. on the 4th nearest stitch of the cluster — 1 tr. at the end of the cluster. — Always 3 ch. between the tr. — 1 tr. with ch. inserted before and after each p. of the arches. — There should be 22 holes. — After the 3rd cluster, t.

*8th row.* — All round on the 22 holes, small scallops; for each. — 1 d. st. — 5 tr. — 1 d. st.

On the edge. — 1 arch into the curve without p. — 1 arch, the d. st. before the nearest p. — 1 arch, the d. st. after the p. in the same curve — then 1 arch on each arch of the previous row — in all 9 arches — the 2 last with st. on the cluster and on the 1st small scallop.

Join 4 scallops to the 4 corresponding scallops of the previous sprig.

DÉMONSTRATION

Fig. nº 15

# Narrow Lace with Serpentine

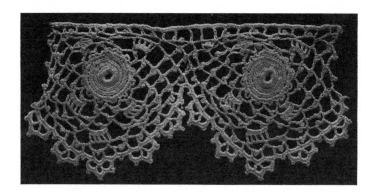

FOUNDATION
CORD :
Cordonnet 6 fils
à la Croix
C·B n° 5

FIG. N° 16

THREAD :
Fil d'Irlande
Brillanté
C·B n° 140

Wind the cord 4 times round the crochet handle and over it work :

*1st row.* — 24 d. st.

*2nd row.* -- Always 1 d. st. worked on the back loop.

*3rd row.* — Alt. — 1 d. st. and 2 d. st. into the folloving st. Always 1 d. st. 3 times — theh 4 ch. and 1 d. st. into the st. where the last st. was worked.

*5th row.* — 1 arch (7 ch. — 1 d. st. into the 3rd st. — 4 ch.) — 1 d. st. on the ring between the p. — Repeat 11 times till there are 12 arches.

*6th row.* — 1 cluster (6 ch. — 1 d. st. into the nearest arch. — T. — 1 ch. — 8 d. st. on the ch. — T. — 4 ch. — 1 tr. on the 2nd d. st. — 1 ch. — 3 times again 1 tr. and 1 ch. on the cluster) — then 2 arches — 1 cluster, 3 times. — There should be 4 clusters.

*7th row.* — Always 1 arch, the d. st. worked after the p. of the nearest arch.

On the cluster — 1 d. st. into the 1st hole ; — for the following arch — 1 d. st. into the last hole — 3 arches between the clusters of the previous row — to finish 2 arches.

$8^{th}$ *row.* — Always arches. — After the $6^{th}$ arch — 1 cluster which forms the point of the scallop — then 6 arches. — T.

$9^{th}$ *row.* — 8 ch. to stand for the $1^{st}$ arch — 1 p. — 4 ch. — Then always arches as previously, the st. worked before the p. of the previous row.

Leave the edge. There should be 14 arches.

Finish off the thread or join to the nearest sprig, with 2 arches on the right and 2 arches on the left. To join — 3 ch. — 1 d. st.

*For the edge.* — 1 tr. — 3 ch. with d. tr. at. the junction of the sprigs.

4 d. st. into each hole.

*For the scalloped side.* — Work 1 tr. before 1 p. — 4 ch. — 1. tr. after 1 p. of each arch.

Then the scalloped p. fig. n° 2.

DÉMONSTRATION

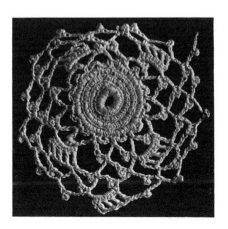

FIG. N° 17

# Baby Irish Lace

## OPEN-WORK DESIGN

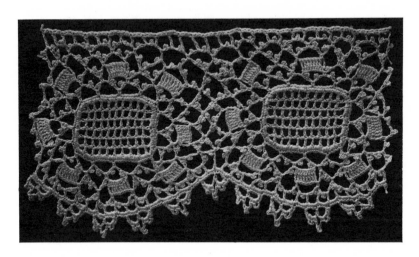

FOUNDATION CORD :  FIG. Nº 18  THREAD :
*Cordonnet 6 fils à la Croix*  *Fil d'Irlande Brillanté*
*C·B nº 5*  *C·B nº 120*

This lace can be made with 1, 2, or several rows. The sprigs worked separately are joined together with crochet, the sprigs being placed between those of the previous row; the centre of a sprig should always be opposite the junction of the 2 sprigs of the previous row.

For a sprig begin by the open squares.

24 ch. — into the 6th st. from the needle, 1 tr. — then always 1 ch. — 1 tr. into the 2nd nearest st. — there should be 20 tr.

To t. — 4 ch. — always 1 tr. on each tr. of the previous row with 1 ch. in between. Work 5 similar rows, that is to say 6 rows of open work in all.

All round on a cord – 3 d. st., even at the corners. Leave the cord.

1st *row*. — 6 ch., join into a p. the last 5 — 6 ch. — join into a p as previously — 1 ch. — then 1 d. st. — this forms a double arch. — Repeat 15 times, it makes 16 arches, 4 on each side long or short.

*2*nd *row*. — 1 double arch — 1 d. st. between the 2 p. of the previous row — then 1 cluster (5 ch., 1 st. into the following arch. — T. — 8 d. st. on the ch. — t. — 4 ch. — 7 tr. on the 7 d. st.) — 6 ch. — join into a p. the last 5 — 1 ch. and 1 d. st. on the arch where the cluster was begun. Repeat. — There should be 8 clusters.

*3*rd *row*. — Always double arches — stick the needle alt. in the middle of the arch of the previous row, then on the st. at the right side of the cluster, then at the left of the same cluster.

The sprig is complete. To join them together, after the 3rd row, work — 6 ch. — 1 d. st. into the 2nd to form the p. — 1 ch. — join with 1 d. st. to the nearest arch which is the one with the cluster of the short side over it — 1 d. st. — 1 p. — 1 d. st. — join to the opposite sprig — keep on joining alt. to one sprig and to the other. You should join 3 times to each sprig.

Then one double arch — 1 d. st. on the nearest arch or the right sprig — 1 double arch — 1 st. on the following arch of the same sprig — 1 double arch. — T. — 1 d. st. on the arch before the last worked previously — 1 double arch — 1 d. st. on the left side, into the arch above the cluster. — Break off the thread.

Finish the scalloped edge with the p. fig. n° 4.

DÉMONSTRATION

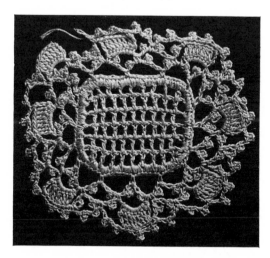

FIG. N° 19

# Fine Lace

## SCALLOPED HORSESHOE

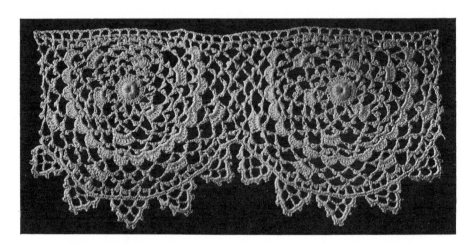

FOUNDATION
CORD :
*Cordonnet 6 fils à la Croix*
*C·B n° 5*

FIG. N° 20

THREAD :
*Fil d'Irlande*
*Brillanté*
*C·B n° 140*

Wind the cord 4 times round the handle of the needle and over it work — 32 tr. — join with 1 tight st. the last to the 1st. — T.

*1st row.* — Always 1 double arch (5 ch — 1 d. st. into the 2nd st. — 5 ch. — 1 d. st. into the 2nd st. — 1 ch.) — stick alt. 1 d. st. into the 2nd and into the 3rd nearest st. of the ring. — There should be 11 double arches in all.

*2nd row.* — 1 double arch — stick between the 2 p. of the arch in the previous row — then 1 cluster (5 ch. — 1 d. st. into the following arch. — T. — 5 ch. — 1 d. st. on the previous st. — 3 ch. — 7 tr. on the 5 st. workeed one way and back) 1 double arch — 1 d. st. into the following st.

2 more double arches — then 1 cluster — that is to say 3 arches after each cluster — repeat twice — there are 3 clusters.

*3rd row.* — Always double arches — stick into the 3 ch. beginning the cluster, then in the middle of the cluster.

*4th row*. — 3 double arches — 1 cluster — 4 double arches — 1 cluster — 4 double arches — 1 cluster — 1 double arch.

*5th row*. As the 3rd row — always double arches — but leave one side to form the edge — the last arch is worked on the st. following the 3rd cluster. — T.

*6th row*. — 7 ch. — 1 d. st. between the 2 p. of the nearest arch — 16 times, 6 ch. — 1 d. st. — stick in the middle of the

DEMONSTRATION

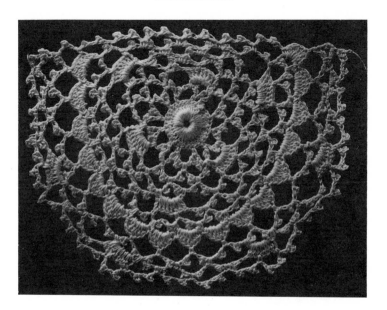

FIG. Nº 21

arch — but to increase and to form the round — in the 5th, 9th and 13th hole stick on each side of the 2 p. of the arch. — T.

*7th row*. — All round on the 17 holes, small round scallops, for each. — 1 d. st. — 6 tr. — 1 d. st.

*8th row*. — Work on the side left for the edge — 6 times 1 double arch — the st. of the 6th arch is worked on the 1st scallop of the horse shoe.

Always 1 double arch, the d. st. worked in the middle of the small round scallop. — T.

*9th row*. — 3 double arches — 1 cluster — 2 double arches — 1 cluster — 3 arches and 1 cluster — 2 arches — 1 cluster — 3 arches. — T.

*10*<sup>th</sup> *row.* — Always 1 double arch as for the 3<sup>rd</sup> row. — Do not work on the edge.

Finish off the thread or join the sprig to a similar sprig.

To join :

5 ch. — 1 d. st. into the 2<sup>nd</sup> st. as for an arch — then 1 ch. — join with 1 d. st. alt. to the sprig on the right side then to the sprig on the left side in the middle of the nearest arch — join 5 times on each side.

For the edge :

*1*<sup>st</sup> *row.* — 1 tr. — 2 ch.

*2*<sup>nd</sup> *row.* — 1 tr. — 2 ch.

For the scalloped side work round :

1 tr. — 2 d. st.

Then the p. fig. n° 6.

# Edging with small Flowers

FOUNDATION
CORD :
*Cordonnet 6 fils
à la Croix*
*C·B n° 5*

THREAD :
*Fil d'Irlande
Brillanté*
*C·B n° 100*

This narrow lace is used to finish off a collar or as a border.
For a small flower.

Work on the cord — 12 d. st. — join into a ring with 1 tight
st. Without the cord — *1 d. st. on the nearest st. — on the
following st. of the ring 5 tr. — repeat 5 times from *.

There are 6 leaflets, end with 1 tight st. — then pass the
needle under the flower to take a thread underneath catching the
cord. — On this cord 6 d. st. — join under the end of the 2nd leaf
— 12 d. st. on the cord.

Always repeat for a flower.

# Narrow Insertion

## REVERSED HORSESHOES

FOUNDATION
CORD :
*Cordonnet*
*6 fils à la Croix*
*C·B n° 5*

FIG. N° 23

THREAD :
*Fil d'Irlande*
*Brillanté*
*C·B n° 140*

This insertion matches the lace : scalloped horse shoe.

Over the cord which has been wound twice round the handle of the needle — 24 tr. — join with 1 tight st. the last to the 1 st.

*1st row.* — Always 1 arch — (5 ch. — 1 d. st. into the 2nd st. — 5 ch.) — 1 d. st. into the 4th st. of the ring. — Repeat 5 times. — There should be 6 arches.

*2nd row.* — 1 arch — 1 cluster — (5 ch. — 1 d. st. before the p. of the nearest arch. — T. — 5 ch. — 1 d. st. on the previous st. — T. — 3 ch. — 7 tr. on the 5 st. worked one way and back) 1 arch. — 1 d. st. after the p. of the arch which has been previously worked into.

2 more arches, then 1 cluster. — T.

*3rd row.* — 5 ch. — 1 tr. on the 2nd tr. of the cluster — 4 ch. — 1 tr. on the 4th tr. of the cluster — 4 ch. — 1 tr. on the last tr. of the cluster — 4 ch. — Always 1 tr. before and after each p., with 4 ch. in between.

*4th row.* — All round on the 13 holes, small round scallops. For each : 1 d. st. — 4 tr. — 1 d. st.

*5th row.* — Work on the side left for the edge — 4 arches — the last is finished on the 1st scallop of the horse shoe.

Always 1 arch — the d. st. worked on the middle of each small round scallop.

Join the sprigs one turned upwards and the next the otherway.

For the junction after the 5th row — 7 ch. — Join to the 4th arch of the nearest sprig — 1 d. st. — then 5 ch. — 1 d. st. into the 2nd one which forms 1 p. — 1 ch. — 1 d. st. on the nearest arch. — Join alt. to the right sprig — then to the left — to finish 5 ch., finish off the thread.

For the edges. — Always 1 tr. — 3 ch. — stick before and after the p. of each arch.

2nd *row*. — 1 tr. into each hole — 3 ch.

DEMONSTRATION

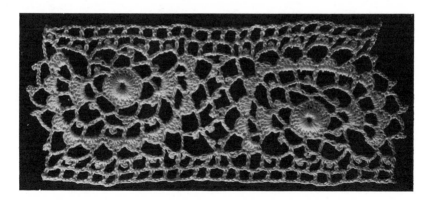

FIG. Nº 24

# Insertion

## WITH FILLING OF ARCHES AND PICOTS

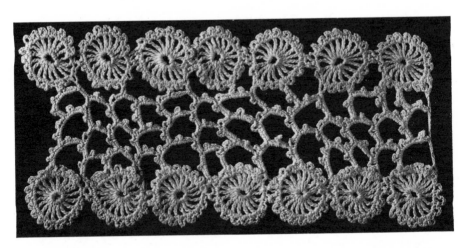

FOUNDATION
CORD :
*Cordonnet 6 fils
à la Croix*
*C·B n° 5*

FIG. N° 25

THREAD :

*Fil d'Irlande
Brillanté*
*C·B n° 120*

Begin with the small wheels.

*For a wheel :*

6 ch. joining the last to the 1st to form a ring.

5 ch. — *1 d. tr. — 1 d. st. — Repeat 16 times from*. — There should be 18 d. tr. — to finish — 1 d. st. into the 4th of the 5 ch.

Between the tr. — always 2 d. st. separated by 4 ch. forming a p.

The 2 last p. of each small wheel are joined to the corresponding 2 p. of the nearest wheel.

When you have the quantity of small wheels required to have an equal length on both sides, baste the wheels on glazed calico or oil cloth. Trace out the pattern so as to have an equal distance between each row. The design shows a straight insertion, but you can trace out a waved insertion or one in a V shape. — This insertion looks very well with a filling of fine Irish Lace.

For the foundation, work 1 ch. from one edge to the other

from right to left. — Then pass the needle under the last wheel and join the working thread on the wrong side, work 5 or 6 ch., to join, always on the wrong side towards the middle of the wheel on the last row.

1 d. st. into 1 of the middle p. — 12 ch. — 1 d. st. on the foundation st. — 4 d. st. — 4 ch. forming 1 p. — 3 d. st.

All the p. are made of 4 ch., by joining the st. it makes 1 p.

12 ch. — Join as previously, then on these ch. — 4 d. st. — 1 p. — 3 d. st

DEMONSTRATION

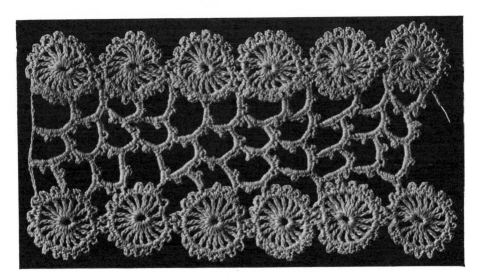

Fig. N° 26

5 ch. — 1 d. st. on 1 p. of the 1st right wheel.

On the 5 ch. — 4 d. st. — 1 p., 3 d. st.

On the free ch, always : 3 st. — 1 p. — 3 st. — 1 p. — 3 d. st.

Each curve usually has 2 p. to separate the d. st.

When you have come back to the right — 1 d. st. into the p. where you began working.

Join the ch. on the wrong side of the work.

In the 2nd row and in the following ones the d. st. which join the arches are worked between the 2 p. of the arches in the previous row.

The arches are not always alike, according to the disposition, work 10 or 12 ch.; and about every 4<sup>th</sup> row miss (at the beginning on the left) 1 arch, to form one at the right of the work.

When the last arch is near a wheel join one of the p. with 1 st. on a p. of the ring. This insertion should not be regular, it would not have its particular character if the rows of arches were worked in straight lines.

# Lattice work Insertion

## WITH DAISY AND STAR

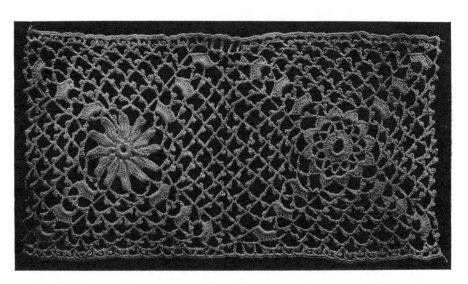

FOUNDATION
CORD :
*Cordonnet*
*6 fils à la Croix*
*C·B nº 5*

FIG. Nº 27

THREAD :

*Fil d'Irlande*
*Brillanté*
*C·B nº 5*

Begin by the sprig of the middle.

*For a Daisy :*

Wind the cord twice round the handle of the needle; over it work: 24 d. st., join the last to the 1st to form a ring.

Over the cord — 12 d. st. — T. — 1 ch. — 12 d. st. on the previous ones. — Work on the back loop to form a rib. — 1 d. st. on the 2nd nearest st. of the ring. — T.

* 1 ch. — 6 d. st. on the 6 nearest st. of the 1st point — 6 d. st. on the cord alone. — T. — 1 ch. — 12 d. st. to form the rib. —

1 d. st. on the ring. Repeat 10 times from *. There are 12 points.

Join the end of the last point to the beginning of the 1$^{st}$.

*1$^{st}$ row*. — Always 1 double arch (for a double arch — 7 ch. — 1 d. st. into the 3$^{rd}$ st. — 7 ch. — 1 d. st. into the 3$^{rd}$ st. — 2 ch.)

DEMONSTRATION

FIG. N$^{o}$ 28

1 d. st. at the end of each point. — To finish the 1$^{st}$ row, only 1 plain arch.

*2$^{nd}$ row*. — * 1 cluster (for a cluster — 8 ch. — 1 d. st. between the 2 p. of the nearest arch. — Work 8 ch. coming back — 1 d. st. — 3 ch. — 9 tr. on the 8 d. st.) then 6 ch. — 1 d. st. after the p. where you began the cluster — 2 double arches.

Repeat 3 times from *.

*3$^{rd}$ row*. — Always double arches — they are worked into the arches of the previous row. — On the clusters, stick the needle before, after, and in the middle of each.

*4*ᵗʰ *row.* — As the 2ⁿᵈ row. — There are 4 double arches between the clusters.

Always double arches as in the 3ʳᵈ row.

*6*ᵗʰ *row.* — As the 2ⁿᵈ row. — there are 6 double arches between the clusters.

*7*ᵗʰ *row.* — As the 3ʳᵈ and 5ᵗʰ rows.

Join one of the sides to the nearest sprig with ch. and p. — join with d. st. alt. on the right and on the left.

A sprig with daisy should alternate with a sprig with star.

The description of the star is given in the sprigs fig. 11 n° 2.

# Waved Insertion

## WHEEL WITH SMALL TRIANGULAR SPRIG

FOUNDATION CORD :
*Cordonnet 6 fils à la Croix*
*C·B n° 5*

FIG. N° 29

THREAD :
*Fil d'Irlande Brillanté*
*C·B n° 140*

Begin with the centre sprig.

For a filled triangle :

On 10 ch. joined into a ring work 28 tr. — the 1st tr. is made of 3 ch.

* 5 d. st. on the 5 nearest st. — 10 ch. — miss 4 ch. of the ring — repeat twice from *.

18 d. st. on the 10 ch. — 5 d. st. on the st. of the previous row.

Always tr. on each st.

*1st row.* — Pass the thread underneath to join at the beginning of the curve — 1 d. st. — 1 arch (that is to say 7 ch. — 1 d. st. into the 3rd st. to form the p. — 5 ch.) — 1 d. st. into the 4th nearest st. — stick 3 times into the 4th st. — and twice into the 5th st. which corresponds to the flat side of the triangle — there should be 14 arches.

*2nd row.* — Always arches — the d. st. is worked after the p. of the previous row.

*3rd row.* — 1 tr. — 4 ch.
The tr. st. are worked before and after the p. of the previous row — there should be 28 tr.

*4th row.* — On the cord — Always 6 d. st. into each hole or space.

*5th row.* — Without the cord — Alway 1 d. st. into the back loop of the st. in the previous row.
Above the p. of the 2nd row work 1 triple p.
For 1 triple p. — 5 ch. — 1 d. st. into the 2nd of these st. —
1 ch. — 1 d. st. into the st. on the ring where you have worked previously. — For the small loop of the middle — : 6 ch. — 1 d. st. worked into the same st. of the ring. — 5 ch. — 1 d. st. into the 2nd st. — 1 ch. — then 1 d. st. to draw the base of the st. worked previously together.
12 d. st. — 1 triple p. — To finish — 6 d. st.

Fig. N° 30

*6th row.* — *
1 arch. — 1 d. st. into the small loop of the middle on the triple p. — 1 arch — 1 d. st. on the 6th nearest st. of the ring. Repeat from *.

*7th row.* — As the 2nd row — arches with d. st. into those of the previous row.
The sprig is completed. — To work it into an insertion join 5 arches to the corresponding arches of the nearest sprig.
For the edges : on each side.
1 tr. — 4 ch. — 1 tr.; — each tr. before and after 1 p. of each arch.

*2nd row.* — 5 d. st. into each hole — 3 st. only into the hollow part of the scallops.

*3rd row.* — 1 d. st. worked into the back loop — after every

5<sup>th</sup> st. — 1 p. of 4 ch. — and 1 st. into the st. where you have already worked the last st.

By working a straight edge on one side, it makes a lace.

The sprigs alone are used as appliqués, they are finished off as shown in the pattern of our demonstration.

The description of the open work triangle is given in the sprigs fig. n° 11.

# Wheel for Appliqué

For the work use :

FOUNDATION

CORD :

Cordonnet 6 fils
à la Croix

C·B n° 5

FIG. ·N° 31

For the work use :

THREAD :

Fil d'Irlande
Brillante
C·B n° 100,
120 or 140

Over the cord joined into a ring, work :

$1^{st}$ row. — 18 d. st. — join the last to the $1^{st}$.

$2^{nd}$ row. — 4 ch. — 17 tr. separated with 1 ch. — join with
1 tight st. to the $3^{rd}$ of 4 ch.

$3^{rd}$ row. — Into 1 hole 2 d. st. — then 1 d. st. — 4 ch. to form
1 p. — 1 d. st. into the $2^{nd}$ hole. Repeat.

$4^{th}$ row. — 1 arch — (7 ch. — 1 d. st. into the $3^{rd}$ st. — 4 ch.)
— 1 d. st. on the ring between the p. — There should be
9 arches.

$5^{th}$ row. — 1 tr. before the p. of each arch in the previous row
— 4 ch. — 1 tr. after the same p. — 4 ch.

$6^{th}$ row. — Take the cord again — 5 d. st. into each hole.

$7^{th}$ row. — Without the cord. — Into the back loop of the st.
in the previous row always 1 d. st. — In the middle of each group
1 p. of 4 ch. joined with 1 d. st.

# Star with five Leaves

FOUNDATION
CORD :

*Cordonnet 6 fils
à la Croix*
*C·B nº 5*

⚜

THREAD :

*Fil d'Irlande
Brillanté*
*C·B nº 120*

FIG. Nº 32

This kind of star is very much used for appliqués.

The centre and the leaves are worked separately.

*For the centre.* On the cord wound twice round the handle of the crochet needle :

*1st row.* — 30 tr.

*2nd row.* — Working into the loop before the st. of the previous row always — 3 ch. — 1 d. st. into each 2nd st.

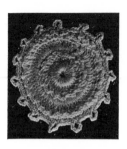

FIG. Nº 33

*3rd row.* — With the cord and into the back loop of the tr. in the 1st row, always 1 d. st.

*4th row.* — Always 2 tr. into each st.

*5th row.* — As the 2nd row.

*6th row.* — As the 3rd row.

*7th row.* — Always work p. separated by 5 d. st. — The 1st of these 5 st. is worked into the same st. which has been worked into before the p.

For a leaf. Over the cord wound twice round the handle of the crochet needle, work :

— 42 —

*1ˢᵗ row.* — 18 d. st.

*2ⁿᵈ row.* — 1 arch (7 ch. — 1 d. st. into the 3ʳᵈ st. — 3 ch.) — 1 st. into the 3ʳᵈ nearest st. of the ring. Repeat 5 times — that is to say 6 arches.

*3ʳᵈ row.* — Always arches, the d. st. worked before the p. of the arch in the previous row.

*4ᵗʰ row.* — Always arches, with st. worked before and after the p. 4 times — there should be 7 arches — then twice 1 arch with st. before the p.

*5ᵗʰ row.* — 1 arch — 1 tr. after the same p. where you have worked previously the last d. st. — Always 4 ch. — 1 tr. before and after the p. — Work 15 tr. — T.

*6ᵗʰ row.* — With the cord — 5 d. st. into each hole. — T.

*7ᵗʰ row.* — Without the cord — 5 d. st. — 1 p. of 4 ch. on each 3ʳᵈ st. of each group. — T.

*8ᵗʰ row.* — Always arches with d. st. worked between the p. — T.

*9ᵗʰ row.* — Always arches, the d. st. are worked before the p. of the arches in the previous row.

The 2 last arches are joined to the corresponding arches of the nearest leaf.

When the 5 leaves are made and joined together, draw the base to sew them under the filled centre.

DEMONSTRATION

FIG. Nº 34

# Star with five Leaves

## AND SMALL ROSE

FOUNDATION
CORD :

*Cordonnet 6 fils
à la Croix*
*C·B n° 5*

❧

THREAD :
*Fil d'Irlande
Brillanté*
*C·B n° 120*

FIG. N° 35

The centre of the star is a small rose made as the one in the scalloped lace with p. fig. 14.

There are 4 rows of small leaves and 6 leaves in each row.

The last leaves are made of : 1 d. st. — 9 tr. — 1 d. st.

Around, work : — 1 row of double arches or :

7 ch. — 1 d. st. into the 3rd st. to form the p. — 7 ch. — and 1 d. st. into the 3rd st. — then 3 ch. — Work each time 1 d. st. after 1 arch. — The d. st. are worked into the 3rd, 6th, and 9th st. of each small leaf of the rose.

There should be 18 arches. Break off the thread.

Work each leaf of the star separately.

For a leaf. — Over the cord wound 3 times round the handle of the crochet needle, work :

*1*<sup>st</sup> *row.* — 26 d. st. — join the last st. to the 1<sup>st</sup>.

*2*<sup>nd</sup> *row.* — 1 arch, or: 7 ch. — 1 st. into the 3<sup>rd</sup> st. to form the p. — then 2 ch. — 1 d. st. into the 4<sup>th</sup> st. of the ring. Repeat.

*3*<sup>rd</sup> *row.* — Always arches — the d. st. is worked before the p. of the arch in the previous row.

On the 7<sup>th</sup> arch after the p., work 1 ch. and join with 1 d. st. to 1 of the arches around the centre rose — then 2 ch. — 1 d. st. the nearest arch of the leaf.

2 ch. — 1 d. st. into the arch following the one into which you worked round the rose.

*4*<sup>th</sup> *row.* — 4 ch. on the leaf — 1 tr. after the nearest p. — 4 ch. — 1 tr. before and after the p. separated by 4 ch. 2 tr. sepa- rated by 4 ch. before the p. — Keep on working the tr. with 4 ch. — 3 times 1 tr. — then 2 tr. on the same st. — 4 times 1 tr. then 4 ch. — 1 d. st. on the nearest arch round the rose. — T.

*5*<sup>th</sup> *row.* — Join the cord into a loop so that the end will not show. Always 5 d. st. into each hole. — T.

*6*<sup>th</sup> *row.* — Working on the back loop — 25 d. st. — T. — 3 ch. joined by a d. st. on the 5<sup>th</sup> st. — 9 d. st. on the loop formed by the 5 ch.

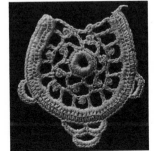

Fig. N<sup>o</sup> 36

18 d. st. on the leaf - T. — 5 ch. joined with 1 d. st. to the 5<sup>th</sup> st. — 5 ch. joined to the 5<sup>th</sup> st. — T. — 9 d. st. on the 5 first ch. — 4 d. st. on the following loop. — T. — 5 ch. — 1 d. st. joined on the 5<sup>th</sup> st. of the 1<sup>st</sup> small ring — T. — 9 d. st. on the loop at the top, and 5 d. st. on the 2<sup>nd</sup> part of thes mall loop at the base.

13 d. st. on the leaf. — T. — 1 small loop as previoulsy, or: 5 ch. with 5 d. st. worked over them.

Keep on working the d. st. on the leaf, then cut the cord and break off the thread.

When all the leaves are made, join with a needle on the wrong side each leaf to the nearest on a length of about 20 st.

# Yoke of old fashioned Irish Lace

FOUNDATION CORD :
*Cordonnet 6 fils à la Croix*
C·B n° 5

FIG N° 37

THREAD :
*Fil d'Irlande Brillanté*
C·B n° 100

This kind of lace is absolutely different trom classical Irish Lace.

It is a handsome work, and is the reproduction of old pieces. The working is not difficult. The sprigs are made separately, then joined together by a filling of ch. and p.

Each sprig is made of a heavy and open work wheel, forming the centre with 3 flowers. The flowers usually have 5 small leaves, some only have 3. For the joining, a flower must sometimes be omitted, and sometimes a detached flower is used; you can thus work the shape you wish.

All sprigs are begun in the same way.

Over the cord wound 3 times round the handle of the crochet needle or on a very narrow net mesh, work :

*1st row.* — 24 d. st. worked very tightly — join the last to the 1st with a tight st.

*2nd row.* — Without the cord — but leaving it underneath — 3 ch. — 1 d. st. into the 2nd nearest st. of the ring — repeat 11 times.

*3rd row.* — As the 2nd row, the d. st. is worked into the holes of the previous row.

$4^{th}$ *row*. — With the cord — 4 d. st. into cach hole of the previous row.

$5^{th}$ *row*. — Always with the cord. — Work on the back loops of the d. st. — 16 d. st. increasing 1 st. every $4^{th}$ st. Begin a flower.

T. — For the centre of the flower, work over the cord 15 d. st. — join into a ring the 12 last by working 1 st. into the edge — 1 ch.

For a leaf :

Over the cord. — 1 d. st. — 1 slip — st. — 12 tr. — 1 d. st. — T. — 1 d. st. on each. st. — work always into the back loop to form the rib.

2 d. st. on the 2 nearest st. of the ring — then 1 ch. — T.

For the $2^{nd}$ leaf :

With the cord — 6 d. st. on the 6 nearest st. of the $1^{st}$ leaf — 10 st. on the cord only.

Leave the cord. — T. — 2 ch. — 1 d. st. on the $2^{nd}$ nearest st. to the end of the leaf. — T. — 2 ch. — 1 d. st. into the nearest hole. You are back at the point of the leaf — 1 d. st. on the last st. of the 10 st. — T. — 1 ch. — Take the cord again. — 1 d. st. on the st. just worked — 3 d. st. into the $1^{st}$ hole — then 2 d. st. into each hole — 2 d. st. on the 2 nearest st. of the small ring — 1 ch. — T.

Form the point of the leaves and the round part neatly, draw the cord when working.

For the $3^{rd}$ leaf :

With the cord. — 6 d. st. on the 6 nearest st. of the $2^{nd}$ leaf — 12 st. on the cord only. — T. — Without the cord. — 1 ch. — then always on the back loop : 1 d. st. — 1 slip — st. — 12 tr. — 1 slip — st. — Break off the thread.

With the cord begin again at the point of the leaf. — Always 1 d. st. on the back loop. To form the round part work 2 st. into the $4^{th}$ st. from the point. Miss tr. st. on the d. st. made previously. 2 d. st. on the small ring — then 1 ch. — T.

For the $4^{th}$ leaf :

With the cord — 8 d. st. on the 8 nearest st. of the $3^{rd}$ leaf — 8 st. on the cord only.

Keep on working as the $2^{nd}$ leaf — going and back one row of open spaces. Take the cord again — 1 d. st. — 3 d. st. into the $1^{st}$ hole and 2 d. st. into the following holes. — 2 d. st. on the small ring — 1 ch. — T.

For the $5^{th}$ leaf :

With the cord — 6 d. st. on the 6 nearest st. of the $4^{th}$ leaf — 10 ch. on the cord only — T.

Without the cord — 1 ch. — 1 d. st. — 1 slip — st.    10 tr. — 1 slip — st. Break off the thread.

Join to the point of the leaf and work with the cord as for the 3rd leaf — always d. st. — 2 d. st. on the small ring — keep on working d. st. on the following st. — Then round the circle 18 d. st. increasing 1 st. every 4th st.

Begin the 2nd flower.

As the 1st, but only 12 d. st. of which the last 10 are joined into a ring :

On the 4th leaf work :

With the cord — 4 d. st. on the st. of the previous row — 12 st. on the cord only. — This flower is more apart, it is finished as usual.

At the end of the 2nd flower always d. st. on the ring — then on the circle — join the beginning to the last row.

Work a 3rd flower.

For the 1st leaf :

Over the cord — 12 d. st. — T. — Without the cord. — After 1 ch. — 1 d. st. — 1 slip — st. — 8 tr. — 1 slip — st. — Break off the thread. — Finish as the 3rd leaf of the 1st flower.

For a small group of 3 flowers after a small ring.

*1st leaf.* — Over the cord — 1 d. st. — 1 slip — st. — 10 tr. — 1 slip — st. — then always d. st.

*2nd leaf.* — (with open work) 5 d. st. on the 1st leaf — 10 st. over the cord — and continue.

*3rd leaf.* — 6 d. st. on the 2nd leaf — 8 st. over the cord, to continue as indicated above.

Raised small rings are sewn on

FIG. N° 38

the small ones which form the centre of the flower, and on the heavy and open worked circle.

For a ring wind the cord 4 times round the handle of the crochet needle and fill it with d. st. worked very closely.

While working draw the st., then on a crochet needle or on a mesh make the ring quite round; the wrong side of the work is the right side of the ring.

To fill these small rings there should be about 25 d. st. Baste the sprigs on glazed calico or oil — cloth on which the pattern has been traced out, and with the same thread, work a filling of ch. and p.

8 ch. — 1 d. st. into the 3$^{rd}$ st. — 3 ch. — join to a leaf. — So as not to break off the thread too often slip ch. under the leaves. — Sometimes work 2 or 4 ch. according to the empty spaces.

# Yoke of old fashioned Irish Lace

FIG. Nº 39

# Small Clover

FOUNDATION
CORD :
*Cordonnet 6 fils
à la Croix*
*C·B n° 5*

FIG. N° 40

THREAD :
*Fil d'Irlande
Brillante*
*C·B n° 120-140*

Begin by the stem.

Over the cord. — 3o d. st.

Over the cord. — For a small leaf* — 1 d. st. — 1 slip — st. — 24 tr. — 1 slip — st. — 1 d. st. — join the last st. to the 1st to close the leaf. Repeat twice from*.

Over the cord. — 20 d. st. — join into a ring for the centre — t. so as to have the ring on the wrong side.

Always over the cord. — 1 d. st. into the back loop of the tr. st. in the previous row which have formed each leaf. In the deep part miss 1 st., and join once to the edge of the small ring.

Work back on the st. of. the stem working the st. into the back loop.

# Tie End

## OLD FASHIONED IRISH LACE

This pretty tie end is the reproduction of an old design, and can be used either to trim a tie or a fancy bow.

It makes a very effective point to appliqué in a blouse, a collar of embroidery or lace.

The sprigs are worked separately.

### N° 1. Wheel for the top

Wind the cord 3 times round a pencil or a net mesh and over it work :

$1^{st}$ *row*. — 42 d. st. — join by 1 tight st. the last to the $1^{st}$.

$2^{nd}$ *row*. — Without the cord. — Always 1 d. st. worked into the back loop of the st. in the previous row.

$3^{rd}$ *row*. — 7 ch. — 1 d. tr. into the $2^{nd}$ nearest st. — 3 ch. — always 1 d. tr. — 3 ch. — after the $20^{th}$ d. tr., work the 3 ch. and join to the $5^{th}$ of the 7 st.

$4^{th}$ *row*. — Take the cord again to work only round the circle* — 4 st. into the nearest hole — 2 d. st. — 5 ch. — 2 d. st. into the $2^{nd}$ hole — 3 d. st. into the $3^{rd}$ hole.

FIG. N° 41

Then 15 ch. — t. and join to the $2^{nd}$ st. of the $1^{st}$ group of d. st. worked round the ring. — T. — 22 d. st. on the 15 ch. — 1 d. st. into the last hole where you have worked. Repeat 6 times from*.

$5^{th}$ *row*. — Without the cord — on the arches of 22 d. st., always working into the back loop of the st. in the previous row. — Leave the $1^{st}$ st. — 1 d. st. on the 6 following st. —

1 p. — (6 ch. — 1 d. st. into the st. where you have worked previously) — 8 d. st. — 1 p. — 6 d. st — Leave the last st. and pass on to the following arch.

———

The side wheels are made exactly the same way, but with 6 arches instead of 7.

Over the cord, work for the 1st row 36 d. st.

For the 3rd row. — 18 tr. instead of 21 d. tr. — do not take the cord again round the circle.

## N° 2. Sprig with point lace stitch

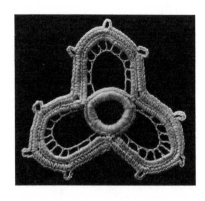

Wind the cord 4 times round a pencil or a net mesh and over it work :

*1st row.* — 60 d. st. worked very tightly.

*2nd row.* — Over the cord only, to form a loop, 44 d. st. — join to the 20th st. of the circle by 1 d. st. — 1 2nd st. on the circle — repeat twice. — There are 3 large loops.

*3rd row.* — Always with the cord — miss the 2 first st. — 10 d. st. working on the back loop of the st. in the previous row — 1 p. (6 ch. — 1 d. st. in the st. where you have worked previously) — 10 d. st. — 1 p. — 10 st. — 1 p. — and 10 d. st. — leave the 2 last st. — Repeat twice.

In the large loops work a point lace st. Tie a very fine thread on the wrong side of the ring, beginning on the left of an open space. — Work a loose button hole st. on the arch — then pass the needle into the loop thus formed — keep on working inside the arch till there are 11 loose st. Then pass the working thread once into each st. to draw in the ring. Finish off the thread.

These st. are worked entirely on the wrong side of the sprig.

## N° 3.  Heavy sprig with treble stitches

Over the cord wound twice round a pencil, work :

*1ˢᵗ row.* — 42 d. st. worked very tightly.

*2ⁿᵈ row.* — Without the cord. — Working on the back loop on the circle — 14 tr. — T. — 2 ch. — miss 1 st. — 10 tr. — miss 1 st. — 1 tr. — T. — 2 ch. — miss 1 st. — 8 tr. — miss 1 st. — 1 tr. — T.

FIG. N° 43

2 ch. — miss 1 st. — 6 tr. — miss 1 st. — 1 tr. — T. — 1 ch. — miss 1 st. — always 1 d. st. — then on the last st. 1 slip — st. — Work down the side with 3 tr. on each side of 1 tr. — 1 tr. into the st. of the circle where you have worked previously.

Repeat the 2ⁿᵈ row twice, and you get a sprig with 3 points of which the angles are rounded.

Round this 3 armed sprig, and forming in a way part of the filling, work always — 1 tr. — 6 ch. — 1 d. st. into the 2ⁿᵈ st. — 2 ch.

## N° 4.  Sprig with long arches

Wind the cord 3 times round a pencil or a mesh and over it work :

*1ˢᵗ row.* — 36 d. st. worked very tightly.

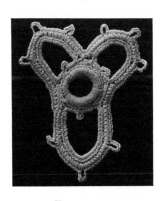

FIG. N° 44

*2ⁿᵈ row.* — 4 d. st. — 1 p. (5 ch. and 1 d. st. into the same st. of the ring) — 4 d. st.

24 ch. — join by 1 d. st. to the 4ᵗʰ st. after the p. — You may t. or join by working in the back with the crochet.

On the ch. — 36 d. st. — 1 d. st. into the st. of the circle where you have worked previously — 6 d. st. on the circle.

Then 3 d. st., 1 p., 3 d. st.

*18 ch. — t. and join to the 3ʳᵈ st. after the p. — T. — On the ch. — 26 d. st. — 1 d. st. into the last st. where you have worked previously on the circle. — Repeat once from*.

To finish instead of 4 d. st. — 6 st. on the circle. Take the cord again.

*3rd row*. — Working always on the back loop of the st. of the previous row.

On the large long arch. 9 d. st. — 1 p. (6 ch. — 1 d. st. into the same st.) — 9 d. st. — 1 p. — 9 d. st. — 1 p. — there should be 3 p. — then to finish 9 d. st. Miss the 1st st. after the arch — 6 st. on the circle — miss the last st. On a small arch.* 7 d. st. — 1 p. — 6 d. st. — 1 p. — 6 d. st. — 1 p. — and 7 d. st.

Between the 2 small arches only 1 d. st. on the circle.

Repeat once from* and to finish 6 d. st. on the circle.

---

When the sprigs are finished baste them on glazed calico or oil-cloth, then work the filling with a finer thread.

For the filling it is not possible to give precise directions as for the sprigs, for you should join to the nearest p., according to the distance. This filling is made with 7 ch. — 1 d. st. into the 3rd st. — 4 ch. — 1 d. st. to join.

# Tie End

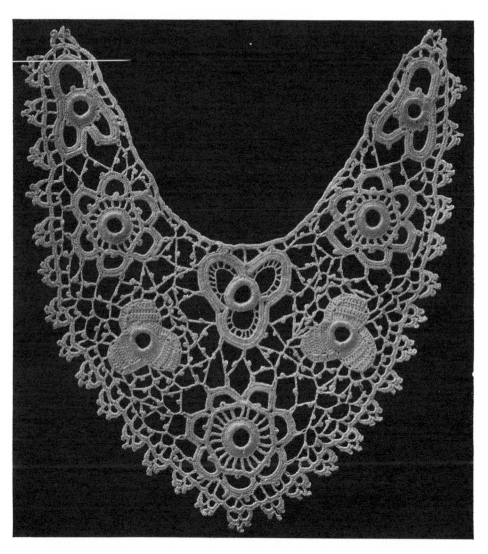

FOUNDATION
CORD :
*Cordonnet 6 fils
à la Croix*
*C·B nº 5*

FIG. Nº 45

THREAD :
*Fil d'Irlande Brillanté*
Springs and picots :
*C·B nº 140*
Filling : *C·B nº 160*

# Sprig with three Points

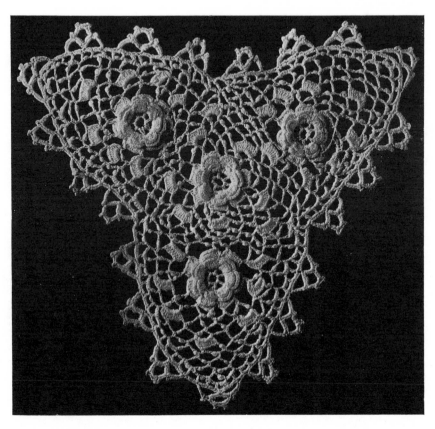

FOUNDATION
CORD :

*Cordonnet 6 fils à la Croix*
*C·B n° 5*

FIG. N° 46

THREAD :

*Fil d'Irlande*
*Brillanté*
*C·B n° 120*

To trim dresses, blouses, etc.

This design is made of small roses (lace with scallops without p., fig. n° 14). Round the roses work arches with p. and clusters. This filling is made of arches (fig. n° 11 of the 1st album " How to make Irish Lace ")* which join the different parts of the designs together.

P. forming the edge (fig. n° 12 — 1st Album)*

*See Publisher's Note

# True Lovers Knot

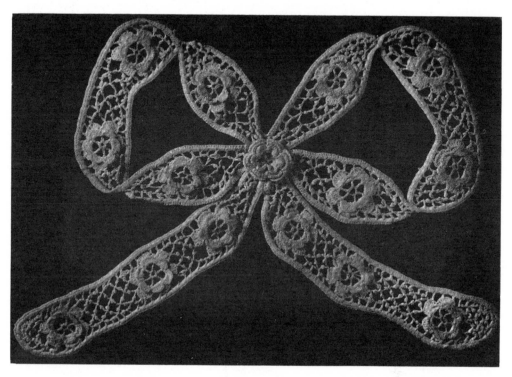

FOUNDATION
CORD :
*Cordonnet 6 fils à la Croix*
*C·B n° 5*

FIG. N° 47

THREAD :
*Fil d'Irlande*
*Brillanté*
*C·B n° 140*

This is used as appliqué in a blouse, or a dress and is very effective.

Small roses (scalloped lace with p. fig. n° 14) are joined together by a filling of d. st. with p. forming insertion.

The pieces of the insertion worked separately are basted on calico or oil-cloth according to the given pattern.

Around the work a cord covered with d. st. worked into the holes of the insertion.

The cord, worked over, follows the outline and goes from one side to the other by folding either on the wrong side or on the right.

In the middle of the bow a rose.

# Collar

# Fancy Tab

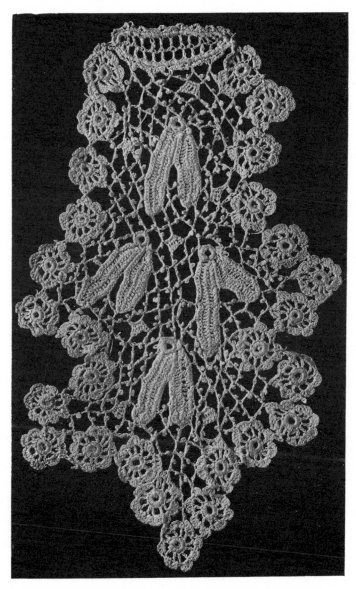

FOUNDATION
CORD :
Cordonnet 6 fils à la Croix
C·B n° 5

FIG. N° 49

THREAD :
Fil d'Irlande
Brillanté
C·B n° 140

# Tab

FOUNDATION CORD :

*Cordonnet 6 fils à la Croix*

*C·B n° 5*

FIG. N° 50

THREAD :

*Fil d'Irlande Brillanté*

*C·B n° 140*

# Bib

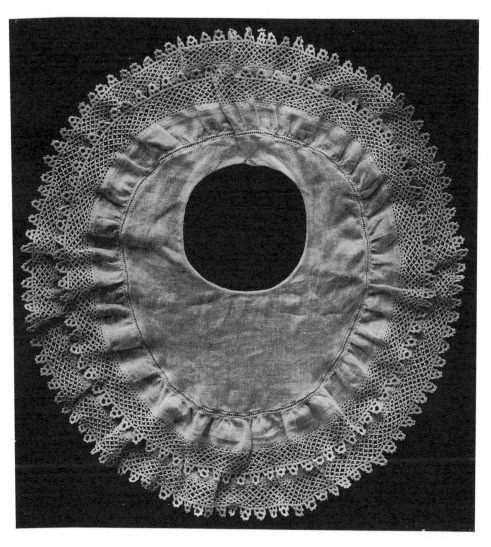

*The lace of this bib is worked with the Fil d'Irlande Brillanté C·B nº 140.*